The MAILBOX®

We ♥ Numbers, Colors, & Shapes

125 fun and practical early math activities!

- Group-time activities
- Center-time ideas
- Small-group activities
- Songs and chants
- Art experiences
- Games and more!

Managing Editor: Kelly Conroy Robertson

Editorial Team: Becky S. Andrews, Margaret Aumen, Diane Badden, Tricia Kylene Brown, Kimberley Bruck, Karen A. Brudnak, Kimberly Brugger, Catherine Caudill, Pam Crane, Chris Curry, Roxanne LaBell Dearman, David Drews, Brenda Fay, Ada Goren, Karen Brewer Grossman, Tazmen Fisher Hansen, Marsha Heim, Lori Z. Henry, Cindy Hoying, Gerri Primak, Mark Rainey, Greg D. Rieves, Rebecca Saunders, Donna K. Teal, Sharon M. Tresino, Zane Williard

TheMailbox.com

 ©2014 The Mailbox® Books
All rights reserved.
ISBN 978-1-61276-482-5

Table of Contents

What's Inside

Five different ways
to learn about each
number, color, and shape!

1

My Circle!
Youngsters learn some basic characteristics of circles as they sing this toe-tapping tune. To begin, give each child a colorful sheet of paper and have her draw a point in the center of it. Then demonstrate how to draw a curved line around the center point, emphasizing how the two ends of the curved line meet up. Guide each youngster to draw a circle around the center point on her paper in the same manner. Then have students cut out their circles. Lead students in singing the song shown, encouraging them to use their circle cutouts to point out the characteristics of circles mentioned in the song.

(sung to the tune of "Clementine")

Oh, my circle!
Oh, my circle!
Oh, my circle, round and neat!
You keep curving round the middle,
And your two ends always meet!

2

Pretty Prints
Students make circle prints of all different sizes at this art center! In advance, gather a variety of items that make a circle print, such as cardboard tubes; paper cups; jar lids; or clean, empty shampoo bottles. Place the items at a center along with paper and shallow containers of paint. A child chooses an item and dips the rim in a container of paint. Then he gently presses the rim of the item on the paper. He continues in this manner using different items and different colors of paint until a desired effect is achieved. When each child is done with his project, challenge him to count the number of circle prints he made on his paper.

Circle

42   We ♥ Preschool: Numbers, Colors, & Shapes • ©The Mailbox® Books • TEC61428

3

Point It Out
Students learn to recognize circles when they participate in this small-group activity! Display several large shape cutouts, making sure that a few of the shapes are circles. Review the shape names with a small group of students. Then lead the group in the chant shown. At the end of the chant, invite a volunteer to point to a circle. If she is correct, remove the circle she pointed to. Continue in this manner with different volunteers until all of the circles have been located. For an added challenge, display circles of various sizes and colors. Include a descriptor in the chant, such as "Point to a small circle" or "Point to a red circle." Then have students find the circle that matches the description.

Circle

Where is a circle?
Where can one be?
Point to a circle
So we can all see!

4

Sweet Circles
Yum! Sorting shapes has never been more delicious! At a center, place a muffin tin and a supply of craft foam shapes. Ensure that there is exactly one circle for each section of the muffin tin. A child visits the center and looks through the shapes. When he finds a circle, he puts it in a section of the muffin tin. He continues until he has placed one circle in each section of the muffin tin. For added fun, have the child pretend to bake the treats and then "serve" them to his classmates.

5

Hop, Jump, or Crawl!
Encourage students to get moving with this gross-motor activity! Gather students in an open area, making sure there is plenty of space between each child. Then announce an action (see the suggested movements) and encourage each student to move his body in a small circle using the action given. Continue in this manner, announcing several different actions for students to perform. To conclude the activity, direct youngsters to join hands to form a large circle.

Suggested movements: spinning, hopping, walking forward, walking backward, jumping, crawling, skipping, stomping

We ♥ Preschool: Numbers, Colors, & Shapes • ©The Mailbox® Books • TEC61428   43

Plus helpful reproducibles!

Oh, Oh, Zero

Youngsters practice number recognition with this little ditty and the accompanying activity! Label blank cards with desired numbers, making sure to label several cards with zero. Display a zero card and lead youngsters in singing the first verse of the song shown. Then display a different card and lead students in singing the second verse. Display each remaining card in turn, prompting little ones to sing the appropriate verse each time.

(sung to the tune of "Skip to My Lou")

Oh, oh, that's a zero.
Oh, oh, that's a zero.
Oh, oh, that's a zero—
The number that means none!

Oh, oh, that's not a zero.
Oh, oh, that's not a zero.
Oh, oh, that's not a zero.
Show us another one!

Berry Picking

Help your hungry bear cubs learn the concept of zero with this cute activity! Give each child (bear cub) in a small group ten red pom-poms (berries) and a bush-shaped cutout. Direct each bear cub to place the berries on the bush. Then recite the rhyme shown, prompting each little cub to pick a corresponding number of berries from his bush and pretend to gobble them up. After confirming that each cub has "eaten" the appropriate number of berries, have him set them aside. Continue in the same way, altering the number of berries, until each cub has zero berries remaining on his bush.

Little bear cubs, hungry for lunch,
Eat [number] berries. Munch, munch, munch!

Who Has It?

To prepare this small-group game, gather number cards from 0 to 10. Direct a volunteer to cover her eyes and stand in front of the group. Then give each child a number card, ensuring that a child gets the zero card. Lead the group in the chant shown; then prompt the volunteer to uncover her eyes and guess which child is holding the zero card. Direct that child to display her card and have the group confirm whether the number is a zero or not. If the number is a zero, lead students in a round of applause. If it is not, encourage the volunteer to name different students until the zero is revealed.

The number zero, it means none.
Try and find it for some fun!

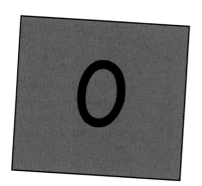

Zooming In on Zero

Little ones practice number identification and formation at this center! Make an oversize masking tape zero on the floor in an open area. Place on the zero small die-cut or craft foam numbers, making sure several of them are zeros. A child walks along the big zero, pausing to pick up each smaller zero along the way. Each time she picks up a zero, she says, "Zooming in on zero!" After returning to her starting position, she replaces the zeros to ready the activity for the next child.

Cookie Snatchers

Students see what zero means when all these cookies disappear! Display a baking tray with five cookie cutouts and lead the group in counting the cookies. Then invite five students to be cookie snatchers. Lead the group in reciting the first two lines of the rhyme. At the appropriate time, prompt a cookie snatcher to take one cookie and return to his seat. Continue with the remaining cookie snatchers, inserting the appropriate number each time. When there are no cookies left, lead the group in saying the last two lines, emphasizing the word *zero*.

[Five] yummy cookies, cooling on the tray.
[Child's name] took one and ran away!

Zero cookies left cooling on the tray.
We'll make cookies another day!

There's Just One

Give each child a number 1 card. Then lead youngsters in singing the song shown, prompting them to display their cards each time the word *one* is sung. As a follow-up activity, lead students in discussing other things of which there are only one.

(sung to the tune of "Three Blind Mice")

Number one. Number one.
There's one Earth and one sun.
There's just one you, and there's just one me.
We are all different, as you can see.
We each have one heart that beats steadily.
The number one.

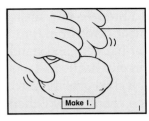
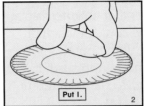
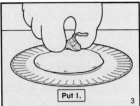

Candy Kiss Cookie

This center activity gives youngsters plenty of practice with the number 1. At a center, place vanilla-scented play dough (cookie dough), a paper plate, an aluminum foil candy kiss shape, and a copy of the direction cards on page 54. Review the cards, pointing out that only one of each supply is needed. A child follows the directions on the cards, making one cookie to place on the plate and then topping the cookie with one candy kiss.

One for One

This center activity provides plenty of practice with number formation! Divide a class supply of paper into fourths; then lightly pencil "1" in each section. Place the papers at a center along with markers, glue, and a variety of items to count, such as pom-poms, cotton balls, craft feathers, and craft foam shapes. A child uses a marker to trace each number on a paper; then he glues one item in each section, saying, "One [item name] for the number one."

One

That's number one — the game is done!

Game Over or Not?

To prepare for this number-identification game, randomly arrange number cards from 0 to 10 facedown in a pocket chart. Lead youngsters in saying the chant. Then invite a child to take a card from the chart and show it to the group as she asks, "Is this the number one?" If it is, lead youngsters in saying, "That's number one— the game is done!" and rearrange the cards for another round. If the number is not 1, prompt youngsters to say, "No way, let's play!" Then set the card aside and continue play.

We're looking for the number one.
When it's found, the game is done!

I Spy!

Invite youngsters to use their hands as binoculars for this game! Ensure that the number one is displayed several times in the classroom, attaching number cards to walls or displays as needed. Then encourage each child to peer through her hands, as if they were binoculars, to find an example of the number 1. When a child spots a number 1, she calls out, "I spy number one!" To confirm that she's correct, have her point to the number that she spied. Repeat the game as desired, encouraging youngsters to find a different example of the number 1 during each round.

Now There Are Two!

For this whole-group pocket chart activity, cut apart copies of the cards on page 55 to make a class supply of matching card pairs. (Plan to participate if you have an odd number of students.) Give a card to each student. Ask a child to show his card and say, "I see one [picture name]." Then help him place the card in the pocket chart. Next, say the chant, prompting a child with a matching card to hold it in the air. After confirming a match, have her place the card in the pocket chart beside the matching card. Then lead the class in saying, "I saw one [picture name], but now there are two!" Repeat until all the cards are paired.

I see one [picture name], but that won't do! Who has a match to make it two?

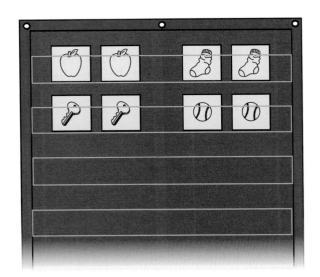

Dip and Trace

Little ones practice number formation with an artistic twist! Set out two shallow containers of different colors of paint and a class supply of die-cut number 2s. Have a child dip her fingertip in one color of paint and then trace a die-cut, prompting her to add more paint to her fingertip as needed. Then have her dip her fingertip in the other color of paint and repeat the process, encouraging her to overlap the colors as desired. As she works, lead her in chanting, "One color, two colors for the number two!"

Dynamic Duos

Students will be thinking in twos for this whole-group brainstorming session! Write the question shown on chart paper. Then read the question aloud. Prompt youngsters to look at themselves and their classmates to jump-start the brainstorming. Then have students name things that come in twos as you write their responses on the chart paper. To extend the activity, help little ones cut out or draw pictures of each twosome and glue it near the corresponding response.

What comes in twos?
ears
eyes
hands
feet
legs
shoes
socks

Two

Marching Along

With this musical activity, youngsters recognize and demonstrate the number 2! Write a large "2" on a sheet of tagboard. Help each child find a partner. Then guide the youngsters to notice that there are two students in every pair. Help the pairs make two lines. Count the lines aloud. Next, play upbeat music and guide the lines to march around the room. Periodically stop the music and have little ones march in place. As they march in place, hold up the number card and lead the group in repeating, "One, two!" for every two steps they take. After a few moments, lower the card and say, "Forward march!" signaling youngsters to march ahead again. Continue as time or student interest permits.

Perfect Pairs

This song and accompanying activity highlight body part pairs and friendship! Invite youngsters to select a partner. Then lead them in singing the song as they perform the actions together. Have students switch partners and lead them in another performance.

(sung to the tune of "Goodnight, Ladies")

Two ears to hear,   *Gently tug your ears.*
Two eyes to see,   *Point to your eyes.*
Two arms to hug,   *Give your partner a hug.*
Two is you and me.   *Point to your partner.*

Two legs to stand,   *Pat your legs.*
Two feet to run,   *Run in place.*
Two hands to wave,   *Wave your hand at your partner.*
Two friends just having fun! *Smile at your partner.*

A Traffic Light Has Three

With this song and activity, youngsters count to three and also learn about traffic lights! Color and cut out a copy of the traffic light pattern on page 56. To begin, hold up the cutout and sing the song, pointing to each light as you count it. Then have students stand a distance from you. Lead them in singing the song again, prompting youngsters to walk fast when they hear "go," slow down when they hear "slow," and stand still when they hear "stop."

(sung to the tune of "The Farmer in the Dell")

A traffic light has three.
Let's count them—one, two, three.
Green, yellow, red, I see.
A traffic light has three.

Green means you can go.
Yellow means go slow.
Red means you'd better stop.
Three things you ought to know!

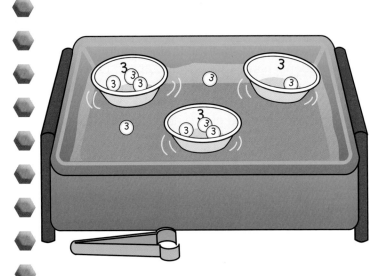

Fill the Bowls

Youngsters practice making sets of three and get a fine-motor workout with this water table activity! Use a permanent marker to label nine Ping-Pong balls and three disposable plastic bowls with "3." Float the balls and the bowls in the table and provide a pair of tongs. A child uses the tongs to pick up and place three balls in each bowl. When she's finished, she counts the balls in each bowl to verify her work and then returns them to the water for the next visitor.

Three Blind Mice

Invite three of your little mice to scurry over to this center to practice number formation! Give each student a copy of page 57 and a small toy mouse (or a gray pom-pom). Instruct each child to place his mouse on the mouse hole. Tell students that the blind mice need help finding the cheese! Then direct each youngster to follow the arrows as he maneuvers the mouse along the number 3 to get to the cheese. For added fun, lead little ones in singing this rendition of "Three Blind Mice" as the mice scurry along to the cheese.

(sung to the tune of "Three Blind Mice")

Three blind mice, three blind mice,
Sniff for the cheese, sniff for the cheese.
They scurry along the number three,
Rounding the curves as quick as can be,
Sniffing for cheese because they cannot see.
Three blind mice, three blind mice.

Where's the Cheese?

Three

That Plate Is Just Right!

To feed these three bears, students will need to find some food! Place at a center grocery circulars, magazines, scissors, glue, a supply of paper plates, and three stuffed bears. A child visits the center, lines up the bears, and counts them. Then she cuts out three food items and glues them on a plate. She then counts the food items to ensure that she has the same number of food items as the number of bears—three!

Leaf Expedition

Students practice counting with this whole-group leaf-hunting expedition! Place around the classroom three leaf cutouts (patterns on page 58) for each child. To begin, tell youngsters they are going on an indoor leaf hunt; then recite the rhyme shown. At the end of the rhyme, instruct each child to find three leaves and bring them back to your group area. Set out a leaf collecting bin and invite each child, in turn, to drop her leaves into the bin one at a time as the group counts them aloud.

We're going on a nature hunt to look for some leaves.
We won't stop looking 'til we each find three!

Pop, Pop, Pop!

Students will be eager to practice number identification with this tasty idea! Label a class supply of popcorn cutouts with numbers, writing "4" on several cutouts. Obtain a bedsheet and a large plastic bowl. Place the bowl in a student-accessible location. To begin, direct each child to hold on to the edge of the sheet while you place the popcorn cutouts in the center. Next, help students shake the sheet vigorously to "pop" the popcorn. Continue until each piece of popcorn falls to the ground. Have each student pick up a piece of popcorn and identify the number. If it is a 4, he places it in the bowl. If it is not, he sets it aside. After the last youngster has identified the number on his popcorn piece, place the popcorn back on the sheet for another round of popping fun!

Fishing for Fours

Float a variety of foam numbers in a water table or a large tub of water. Place a ladle or scooper and a plastic bucket nearby. A child uses the ladle to "fish" for a number. When she finds a number, she determines if it is a 4 or not. If it is, she places it in the bucket. If it is not, she tosses it back in the water. She continues until she has found all the 4s. Then she takes the numbers out of her bucket and verifies that they are all 4s. When she is finished, she returns the numbers to the water to ready the activity for another visitor.

Four

How Many Scoops?

Challenge students to make a quadruple-scoop ice cream cone at this center! Place colorful circle cutouts (ice cream scoops) and brown triangle cutouts (cones) at a center. A child takes a cone and counts out four ice cream scoops. She writes "4" on her cone and then glues the scoops atop the cone.

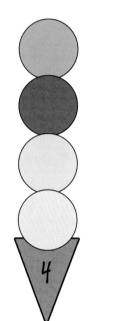

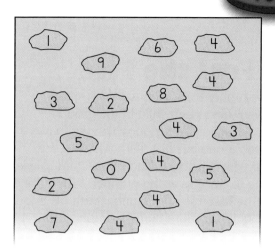

Down the Stream

Little ones learn to recognize the number 4 while participating in this small-group activity. In advance, label a supply of rock cutouts with a variety of numbers, ensuring that the number 4 is written on several rocks. Attach the rocks to a sheet of blue bulletin board paper (stream) so that the rocks labeled "4" make a path down the stream. Tell students that to not fall in the stream, they can only step on rocks labeled "4." Then invite each child, in turn, to walk, hop, or jump on the rocks down the stream. As he lands on a number, have him say it out loud. If he lands on a number that is not four, he "falls in" and his turn is over.

Count Them All!

This song is easy to learn and the accompanying idea gives youngsters practice counting to four! Obtain four stuffed toys and attach a number card (1 through 4) to each toy. Give each toy to a different child and invite the youngsters with toys to stand in front of the group. Lead students in singing the song shown. When each number is sung, direct students to point to the child holding the corresponding stuffed toy. Repeat with different students as desired.

(sung to the tune of "The Farmer in the Dell")

One, two, three, and four.
One, two, three, and four.
Let's count them just once more.
One, two, three, and four!

Feel the Five

Practice number formation with this small-group activity. Give each child in the group a sheet of construction paper on which you have lightly written a number five. Direct him to trace the number with his finger. Then invite him to use colored glue to trace over the number. When the glue is dry, he can trace the number with his finger again and again for more number-writing fun!

How Many Cherries?

Some ice cream sundaes have only one cherry on top, but this special sundae has five! Place copies of the ice cream sundae pattern from page 60 at a center, along with a bowl of red pom-poms (cherries) and a plastic spoon. A child colors his sundae as desired. Then he uses the spoon to get a cherry and places it atop an ice cream scoop. He continues with each remaining scoop. After he places the last cherry on his sundae, he counts the cherries to confirm there are five and then glues each cherry in place.

Note by Note

Students keep their number-recognition skills sharp with this whole-group activity. On the board, draw several music notes. On each note, write a number, including several 5s. Invite a student to come to the board and point to a number 5. Then have him lead the class in making five musical sounds of his choosing—such as ding, boom, or la—as he holds up one finger for each sound he makes. Continue with different students as desired.

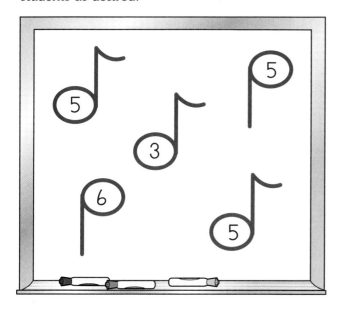

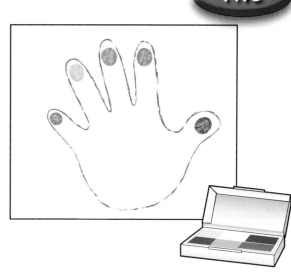

Five

Fingerprint Fun

Youngsters can use these finished projects as counting tools! Gather a small group of students and help each child trace her hand on a sheet of paper. Provide several ink pads for student use. Demonstrate for little ones how to use an ink pad to make a fingerprint. Then, doing one finger at a time, help each child press a finger on an ink pad and make a fingerprint on the corresponding finger of her hand tracing. Finally, lead the group in counting to five, pointing to each finger, in turn, as they count.

Busy Fingers

To begin, have each student hold up one hand. Then lead each student in counting the fingers on her hand. After determining that there are five fingers on one hand, lead students in singing the song shown. As a follow-up activity, direct students to brainstorm other things they can do with five fingers!

(sung to the tune of "The Itsy-Bitsy Spider")

Five fingers on one hand
Are useful, yes, indeed!
I use them when I get dressed
And also when I eat!

They help me do my work
And also when I play.
I use my five fingers
Each and every day!

How Many Sides?

For this counting activity, gather several cube-shaped items—such as a cardboard box, a block, a jumbo die, and a sugar cube—and put all but one item in a bag. Show the item to the group and identify its shape as a cube. Then sing the song shown, leading students in counting the item's six sides at the end of the song. Set the item aside and invite a volunteer to remove an item from the bag. Help the group identify the item; then lead students in singing the song and counting the cube's six sides. Repeat the activity with each remaining item.

(sung to the tune of "Shoo Fly")

A cube has six sides, you see.
Six sides, it has to be.
A cube has six sides, you see.
Please count the sides along with me!

What's in Your Bag?

Little ones partner up and search the room to find sets of six! To introduce this activity, put six pom-poms in a bag. Spill the pom-poms onto the floor and lead the group in counting them to see that there are six. Then challenge students to see how many other sets of six they can make! Assign each child a partner and give each twosome a bag labeled "6." Instruct each pair to find six like items, put the items in the bag, and bring the bag back to your group area. Finally, have each pair, in turn, spill the contents of its bag onto the floor and count the items aloud to verify that the collection is a set of six.

Six

Construction Site

For this small-group activity, give each youngster a different set of six building blocks, such as wood blocks, Lego bricks, and foam blocks. Do not reveal the number of blocks in each set. Encourage each student to use the blocks to build a tower. When the towers are complete, ask youngsters to compare the heights (without counting the blocks). Then lead them in counting the blocks in each tower. Guide students to discover that even though the towers are different sizes, six blocks were used to build each tower.

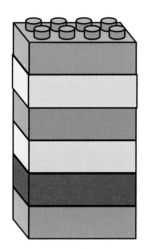

Cubs in Caves

With this center activity, little ones help baby bears find their way home! Set out four cave cutouts, each labeled "6," and provide a collection of 24 bear counters and a jumbo die. Give each child in a group of four a cave cutout. Then tell youngsters that some baby bears got lost in the woods and need help finding their caves. Direct each player, in turn, to roll the die, count the dots, and place that many bears on her cave. If a child's roll would make more than six bears, her turn is over. Play continues until there are six baby bears on each cave.

Oops!

Giggles are sure to abound when you "mess up" this gross-motor activity! Program several cards with directions that focus on six, such as "Do six jumping jacks" or "Hop six times." Take a card and read the directions aloud, emphasizing that the action is to be done *six* times. Lead youngsters in counting aloud as the group performs the action six times; then set the card aside. Repeat with a different card, but this time perform the action and "forget" to stop at six. Little ones are sure to notice your mistake and quickly correct you. After acknowledging your mistake with great silliness, lead students in performing the action the appropriate number of times. Continue the activity, periodically making mistakes and encouraging youngsters to correct you.

Seven Days

This simple song and activity reinforces that there are seven days in a week! Display a calendar and lead students in counting the days of the week. Review the names of the days of the week and then lead youngsters in singing the song shown. For a fun follow-up activity, list the days of the week on chart paper, numbering each one. Then sing the song throughout the week and record a fun event that occurs each day.

(sung to the tune of "London Bridge")

Every week has seven days,
Seven days, seven days—
Seven days to learn and play,
Seven good days!

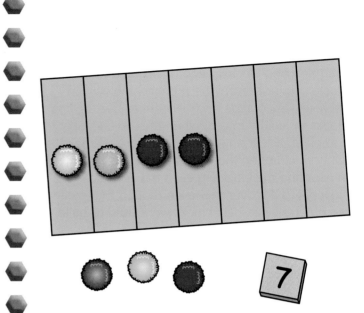

Take a Tile

Number recognition is the key to this partner game. Give each child seven pom-poms and a paper strip programmed as shown. Place a handful of number tiles in a bag, with most of the tiles showing the number 7. Partners take turns picking a tile from the bag. When a tile shows a number 7, the child places a pom-pom on his strip and returns the tile back to the bag. When a tile shows a different number, he returns the tile to the bag and his turn ends. The first player to put seven pom-poms on his strip wins!

Roll the Die

This large-group activity reinforces number identification, counting, and one-to-one correspondence! Label three sides of a cube-shaped box "7" and the three remaining sides with other numbers. Seat students in a circle and hand a child the cube to roll. If the number 7 appears on top, youngsters say, "That's the number seven! What do we do?" Announce a direction such as "Clap your hands seven times" or "Pat your legs seven times." Then lead the group in counting to seven, performing the designated action for each number counted. If a different number lands on top, no directions are given and the child passes the cube to a classmate.

Chunky Numbers

Little ones practice number formation and build fine-motor skills at this center! Attach a large sheet of paper labeled with 7s to a tabletop. Set out a variety of play dough. A child rolls some play dough into a ropelike shape and then forms a number 7 atop one of the numbers written on the paper. She repeats the process until each written numeral is topped with a play dough number.

Lucky Seven

This large-group counting activity has little ones pondering why they're lucky! With students seated in a circle, tell them how seven is often considered a lucky number. Then have youngsters count off from one to seven around the circle, stopping with the classmate who says "seven." Encourage that child to tell the group why he's lucky number seven. For example, a child might say, "I'm lucky number seven because I have a new kitten!" Repeat the counting sequence until each child has had a turn to tell why he's lucky number seven.

Eight Arms

With this song and activity youngsters get a glimpse at what it's like to be an octopus! Have each child hold four crepe paper strips in each hand. (Staple each set of strips together at one end if desired.) Ask her to pretend she is an octopus and that the strips are her eight arms. Then lead youngsters in singing the song shown, encouraging each child to gently move her "arms" as she "swims" about.

(sung to the tune of "Are You Sleeping?")

One, two, three, four,
Five, six, seven, eight
Arms I see, arms I see.

Eight arms like an octopus,
Eight arms like an octopus
Move gently, move gently.

A Figure Eight

Youngsters' fingers do the skating with this number-identification and formation activity! For each child in a small group, use a permanent marker to write a large "8" on a sheet of aluminum foil; then put the foil in a plastic sheet protector (skating rink). Label several cards with numbers, with most of them labeled "8." Set out the rinks and stack the cards facedown. A child flips a card. If the card shows an 8, students say, "Number eight! It's time to skate!" Then each child uses her fingertip to make a figure eight along the 8 on her skating rink. If the card shows a different number, the child's turn ends. Play continues until all the cards are flipped.

Eight

Crawling Along

Little ones practice number formation and strengthen fine-motor skills at this center! Set out play dough, a supply of pipe cleaner halves (spider legs), a toy spider, and a sheet of tagboard labeled with a number 8. A youngster examines the spider and counts the legs. Then he molds play dough to make a spider body and inserts eight legs into the dough. He counts the legs to confirm that there are eight and then "crawls" the spider along the number 8.

From Start to Finish

You'll need plenty of room for this large-group number-recognition game! Get two sheets of tagboard. Label one sheet with a large "8" and the other sheet with a different number. To begin, have students stand behind a start line while you stand a distance away. Announce a gross-motor movement, such as giant steps, baby steps, side steps, or hopping; then hold a card in the air. If the card shows an 8, youngsters move toward you using eight of the designated movements. If the card shows the other number, students stand still. Continue play, randomly showing the cards until everyone reaches you.

Awesome Octopus

Students create a human octopus with this whole-group activity! Display a simple drawing or a picture of an octopus and say, "An octopus is special because it has eight arms." Lead the group in counting the arms and then tell youngsters you'd like to create a human octopus! Invite two children to stand back-to-back and extend their arms; then help the group count their arms to see if there are eight. Repeat with two more children, helping all four students stand with their backs close together and arms extended. After counting to determine that the octopus has eight arms, lead the group in saying the rhyme.

An octopus is special,
With arms that total eight.
For swimming in the ocean,
Eight arms are really great!

I Can Write a Nine

Little ones get plenty of practice writing the number 9 with this simple song and activity! Write "9" on your board. To begin, point to the number and help youngsters identify it. Next, demonstrate how to use your finger to form "9" in the air; then have students do the same. After a few rounds of practice, lead the group in singing the song and air-writing a 9. After the song, invite a volunteer to write "9" on the board next to yours.

(sung to the tune of
"The Farmer in the Dell")

I can write a nine.
I can write a nine.
Draw a circle and then a line.
I can write a nine.

Pop!

Little ones are encouraged to pop balloons with this number-recognition game! Label several balloon cutouts with numbers, writing "9" on most. Lightly attach the balloons to a wall or board and get a pointer. Invite a child to find a balloon that shows a number 9. If he is correct, have him tap the balloon with the pointer. When he taps, encourage the group to say, "Pop!" Then remove the balloon and set it aside. If it's a different number, his turn ends. Continue until all the number 9 balloons are popped.

Nine

Highway Number Nine

Here's a playful way for youngsters to learn how to form the number 9. On a sheet of poster board, draw a large bubble number 9 with dashed lines so it resembles a highway. Provide a paper plate with a thin layer of paint and a toy car. A child dips the wheels of the car in the paint and then "drives" the car along the number, adding more paint to the wheels as needed. As he works, he says, "I'm driving along highway number nine!"

I spy number nine!

Search and Find

Youngsters will love playing this fun number-identification game! In advance, secretly post nine die-cut 9s around the classroom. To begin, display a number 9 and help students identify it. Then tell students that there are nine number 9s hidden around the room and ask them to help you find them. Direct each child who spots one to call out, "I spy number nine!" and point to the number. Each time a 9 is found, collect the die-cut and lead youngsters in clapping nine times. After all nine die-cuts are collected, help students count them to verify that there are nine 9s.

Number Nine Is So Fine!

Invite little ones to play this fun call-and-response number-identification game! Label a supply of cards with numbers, writing "9" on most. To introduce the activity, display a number 9 card and instruct the group to chant, "Number nine is so fine!" Then respond by chanting, "[Clap your hands] and count to nine!" Lead youngsters in clapping and counting to nine; then show a card labeled with a number other than 9 and prompt students to stand quietly. After completing a round of practice, engage little ones in playing the game, inserting a different movement into the response each time a number 9 is shown.

Fingers and Toes

Little ones practice finger and toe counting with this cute song! Invite students to remove their shoes and socks. (Or give each child two die-cut feet.) Demonstrate how to count each finger and thumb as you lead youngsters in singing the first verse of the song, enthusiastically wiggling your fingers at the end. Then lead students in performing the second verse, encouraging each child to wiggle her toes (or die-cut) at the end.

(sung to the tune of "Skip to My Lou")

One, two, three, four, five,
Six, seven, eight, nine, ten,
Ten fingers on my hands.
Ten fingers are just grand!

One, two, three, four, five,
Six, seven, eight, nine, ten,
Ten toes on my feet.
Ten toes are really neat!

Treasure Rings

Little ones make a set of ten and practice one-to-one correspondence at this sensory center! Bury ten small hair bands (rings) in a tub of sand. Place near the tub a container labeled "10." Instruct a child to dig through the sand and find a total of ten rings. As she works, have her place each ring she finds in the container and periodically count the number of rings until she has found ten. After finding all ten, have her slide one ring onto each finger and thumb.

Ten

Catch of the Day!

Youngsters count sets on this small-group "fishing expedition"! Obtain a large bucket and attach a fish cutout to each of ten beanbags. Give each of five students two fish and have the "fishermen" stand a short distance from the bucket. Ask each fisherman to pretend that he caught the two fish; then help the group count all the fish to see that there are a total of ten. Next, have the fishermen take turns tossing the fish into the bucket. Help them count the fish that land in the bucket and on the ground and compare the results. Then lead the fishermen in counting the total number of fish. Point out that, when the sets are combined, the total number of fish is ten. Then redistribute the fish and repeat the activity.

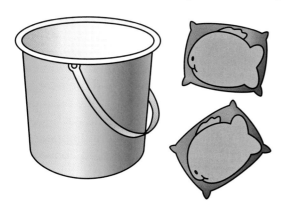

10 9 10

A Perfect Score

Youngsters pretend to be at the Olympic Games during this large-group activity! Invite three "judges" to sit in chairs facing the group. Hand each of two judges a number 10 card and the third judge a number 9 card to hold facedown in their laps. Invite a "competitor" to perform a desired action. Then prompt each judge, in turn, to lift her card and reveal her score. If the score is ten, the crowd yells, "Hip hip hooray!" and claps ten times. If the score is not ten, the crowd says, "Good job!" Then repeat the activity with new judges and a different competitor.

Let's Act Like Hens!

To prepare for this whole-group game, label a supply of cards with numbers, writing "10" on most. Place the cards in a bag and have youngsters stand and face you. To play, take a card from the bag and show it to the group. When the card shows a number 10, have youngsters say, "It's number ten, let's act like hens!" and then strut around pretending to be hens. When the card shows a different number, have students stand quietly.

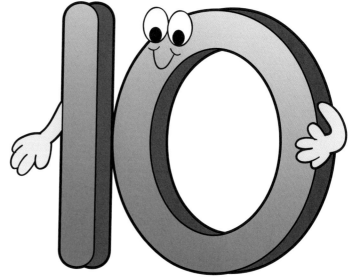

Stop!

Reinforce the color red and street safety with this fun idea! Place a length of bulletin board paper on the floor so it represents a street. Also make a red construction paper stop sign. Lead students in singing the song shown. Then hold the stop sign and have each child, in turn, "cross" the street as you lead him in following the appropriate stop sign procedures.

(sung to the tune of "Up on the Housetop")

Stop signs are red. Oh, yes, indeed.
You must stop for your safety.
Look both directions, and then stay.
Don't cross the street 'til you look each way!

Red, red, red,
Stop signs are red!
Red, red, red,
Stop signs are red!
Stop when you see one. Yes, indeed!
They are so helpful to you and me!

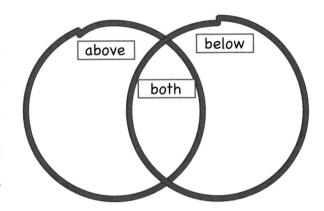

Above, Below, or Both?

Highlight the color red with a life-size Venn diagram! Use yarn to make two oversize, overlapping circles on the floor. Label one circle "above," one circle "below," and the overlapping section "both." To begin, have little ones point to any red they are wearing. Help each student determine if the red she is wearing appears above her waist, below her waist, or both above and below her waist. Then help each child stand in the appropriate section of the diagram. If a child is not wearing red, direct him to stand outside the diagram. After everyone is in place, discuss the results with students.

Designer "Red-Bands"

Instead of headbands, invite your little ones to make these "red-bands." Place at a center a class supply of 3" x 18" red construction paper strips along with a collection of red craft materials, such as pom-poms, feathers, craft foam shapes, sequins, and sticky dots. Invite each child to visit the center and attach desired materials to a strip. When the glue is dry, size the strip to fit the child's head and staple the ends together. Then invite little ones to put on their headwear as you lead them in chanting, "The color red looks good on my head!"

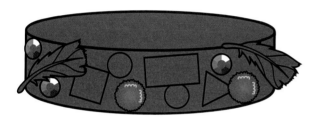

Which Fruit Is Your Favorite?		

Sweet and Tasty!

This sweet activity highlights familiar red fruits and results in a simple graph! Place at a center a class supply of personalized red paper squares and a graph similar to the one shown. Set out strawberry slices, maraschino cherries cut in half, and thin red apple slices. Encourage a few children at a time to join you for a taste test. After a child samples each fruit, have him indicate his favorite one by attaching his square to the appropriate column on the graph. After everyone has added to the graph, discuss the results and see if there is a clear class favorite!

Walk the Circle

Reinforce the color red with this activity! Arrange a class supply of colorful paper, including three or four red sheets, on the floor in a circle. Have youngsters walk along the circle of papers as you say the rhyme shown, prompting students to stop at the end of the rhyme. Ask each child standing on a red paper to name something red. Play several rounds of this game.

Walk on each paper as you go.
Who will stop on red? We'll soon know!

Top the Dots

To make this small-group game, use a blue bingo dauber to make four dots on each of several tagboard squares. Place in a bag four blue pom-poms for each square along with several other colors of pom-poms. In turn, each player takes a pom-pom from the bag. If the pom-pom is blue, he places it atop a dot on his board. If it's a different color, he returns the pom-pom to the bag. The first child to cover all four blue dots says, "Blue-O!" and is declared the winner.

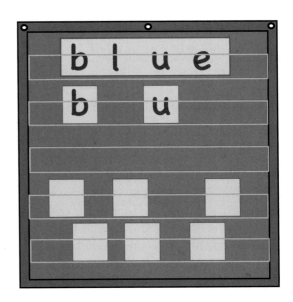

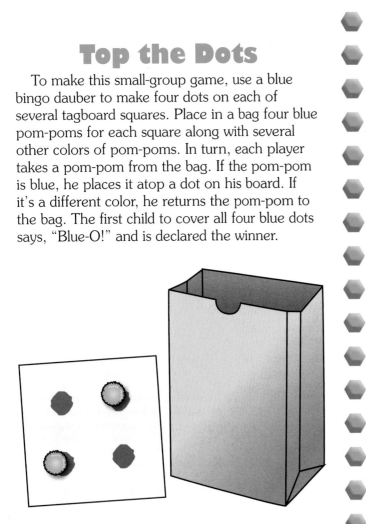

B-L-U-E Spells *Blue!*

Students identify letters and spell the word *blue* with this whole-group activity! Use a blue marker to write the word *blue* on a paper strip. Use the same marker to label a class supply of paper squares with letters, ensuring that the letters *b*, *l*, *u*, and *e* each appear once on four separate squares. Display the strip in a pocket chart and place the squares facedown nearby. Invite a student to take a square and identify the letter. Then point to the strip and ask, "Is the letter [letter name] in the word *blue*?" If it is, have the child place the square below the matching letter. If it is not, have him set the square aside. Continue in the same way until the word *blue* is spelled.

Look Up

All youngsters need for this song and activity are their imaginations! Lead little ones in singing the song shown; then invite each child to tell something he might see when he looks up at a clear blue sky.

**(sung to the tune of
"Row, Row, Row Your Boat")**

Look up at the sky,
Not a cloud in view.
All I see as far as can be
Is the color blue!

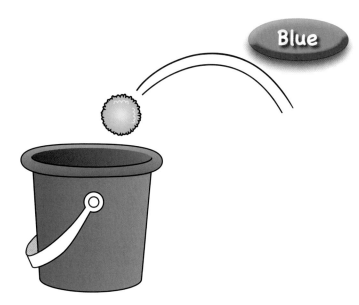

Shoot and Score!

Here's a fun variation of the game of basketball to help your students recognize the color blue! Set out a large blue container and make a masking tape line on the floor several feet away. Place a paper bag with ten large pom-poms (five blue and five other colors) near the line. Invite a small group of children to stand behind the line. Then have a child pick a pom-pom from the bag. If the pom-pom is blue, he tosses it in the container. If the pom-pom is a different color, he does not. When his turn is over, he returns the pom-pom to the bag for the next player. Continue as time allows.

A Colorful Highlight

This large-group game uses colorful streamers, but the highlight is blue! Attach one blue and several other colors of crepe paper streamers to a wall. To begin, point to the blue streamer and have youngsters identify the color. Then invite a volunteer to wear a sleep mask and encourage her to touch the blue streamer. Have her classmates help her by patting the floor quietly when she's near a streamer that is not blue and loudly when she's near the blue streamer. After she's chosen a streamer, have her open her eyes and tell whether the color is blue. After confirming her answer, reattach the streamer to the wall in a new location and invite a different child to play.

Hungry Monkey

Your students are sure to go bananas over this whole-group game! In advance, cut out a class supply, minus one, of colorful bananas, making only one yellow. Gather youngsters in a circle and invite one child to be the monkey. Have the monkey stand in the center of the circle and hide his eyes; then give each remaining child a banana cutout. Lead students in the chant shown. At the conclusion of the chant, have each child hide her banana behind her back. Direct the monkey to uncover his eyes and try to guess which classmate is holding the yellow banana. After he names a child, invite that child to reveal the banana she is holding. If she is holding the yellow banana, she becomes the monkey for the next round and the monkey takes her place in the circle. If she is not holding the yellow banana, the monkey chooses a different child. He continues in this manner until he has found the child holding the yellow banana.

Yellow banana,
Where can it be?
Please, hungry
monkey,
Don't pick me!

A Beautiful Bouquet

Make these craft projects to use as props when singing this delightful ditty! To begin, give each child four yellow tissue paper circles. Help each child staple her tissue paper circles together in the center. Then have each child pull up each tissue paper layer separately and scrunch to form flower petals. Staple a green chenille stem to the bottom of each blossom. Gather youngsters and set out a large plastic vase or plastic cup. Lead students in singing the song, directing each child to hold up her flower as she sings. Then lead students in placing their flowers in the container to make a lovely bouquet!

(sung to the tune of
"The Itsy-Bitsy Spider")

Our yellow flowers
Are pretty as can be!
They grow so tall,
As you can surely see!

Our yellow flowers
Are growing every day.
And soon our yellow flowers
Will make a nice bouquet!

Here Comes the Sun!

Display this finished product to give youngsters a visual reference of things that can be yellow. Label a large yellow construction paper circle as shown. Display the circle and have students identify the color. Then ask students to brainstorm things that are, or can be, yellow. Record each different response on a yellow construction paper strip (ray) by drawing a simple picture of the item. Label each drawing and attach the rays to the circle so that it looks like a sun. Post the sun in an easy-to-see location in the room.

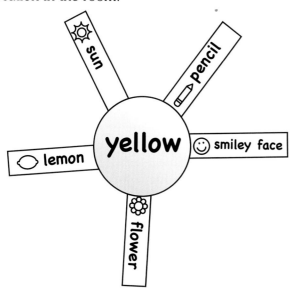

Page by Page

Little ones are sure to read these self-made booklets again and again! For each child in a small group, fold a white sheet of paper in half and then in half again to make a booklet; then title it like the one shown. Provide a supply of magazines, catalogs, and circulars. Invite each child to look for three different pictures of yellow things. When he finds an item, have him cut it out and glue it to one of his booklet pages. When each child is finished gluing his pictures in his booklet, program each page like the ones shown.

Search and Sort

Can your little ones find the hidden yellow items? Invite them to try when they visit this hands-on center! To prepare, partially fill your water table or a large tub with yellow paper shreds. Tuck a variety of yellow items—such as pom-poms, craft sticks, craft feathers, jumbo buttons, and foam shapes—in the paper shreds. Ensure that there are a few of each type of item. A child visits the center and hunts through the paper to find the yellow items. After she finds the items, she sorts the objects by type. If desired, invite each child to explain her sorting rule to you.

A Purple Book

Singing this simple song gets students thinking about other things that are purple! After leading students in singing the song, help them name other things that are purple as you list their ideas on a sheet of chart paper. Then invite each child to choose an item and draw it on a sheet of paper. Help each child label her drawing. Finally, bind the completed drawings into a class book titled "Things That Are Purple."

(sung to the tune of "Hush, Little Baby")

Purple is a color that you just might see,
And purple is a color that is fine with me!
There are purple plums and violets too.
To make this color, mix red and blue.

Great Grapes!

The result of this activity is a big bunch of purple grapes! To prepare, repeatedly trace a circle template on a sheet of tagboard so that the tracings resemble a bunch of grapes. Then use the same template to make a class supply of different-colored paper circles, ensuring there are as many purple circles as there are grapes in the bunch. Place the paper circles in an opaque container and display the tracing for a small group of students. Invite a child to pick a circle from the container and determine whether it is purple. If it is purple, he places it on one of the grapes. If it is not purple, he sets it aside. Continue with each student or until the entire bunch of grapes is purple.

Follow the Path

Youngsters practice purple recognition with this activity. In an open area, use clear Con-Tact covering to attach a variety of colored construction paper squares to the floor, ensuring there is a path of purple squares. A child steps on only the purple squares, saying the color word as he steps on each square. Encourage students to follow the purple path again, this time by hopping, jumping, or tiptoeing.

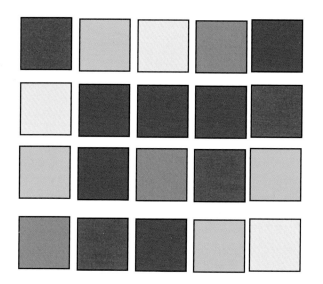

Where Is It?

Students' observation skills are the key to this small-group activity! Gather three paper cups and three objects that can fit under the paper cups making sure that one of the objects is purple. Place each of the objects under a different cup, encouraging students to pay close attention to where you place the purple object. Then slide the cups around, making sure to keep the objects covered. As you move the cups, remind students to keep their eyes on the cup that is covering the purple object. After moving the cups several times, invite a volunteer to lift the cup she believes is hiding the purple object. If she is correct, have her hide the items and move the cups for the next round. If she is incorrect, invite a different child to try to find it.

Hidden Colors

Your students will want to play this small-group game again and again! In advance, glue black construction paper squares and colored construction paper squares back-to-back. Ensure that there are several purple squares made in this manner. Then arrange the squares (colored side down) in a circle on the floor in your group area. Invite each child to stand behind a square. Play soft music and invite students to slowly walk around the outside of the squares. When you stop the music, direct each child to stop by the nearest square and pick it up. Have each child, in turn, display her square and identify the color. Each child who is not holding a purple square sits in the middle of the circle for the next round of play.

Bat Signal

Little ones are sure to enjoy this action-packed color-recognition activity! Gather color cards (one of them black) and designate a certain area of the room to be a bat cave. Instruct your colony of bats to stand in the cave; then display one of the cards. If the card is black, the bats fly once around the room and back to the cave. If it's a different color, the bats stay in the cave. Repeat for several rounds, randomly showing the cards each time.

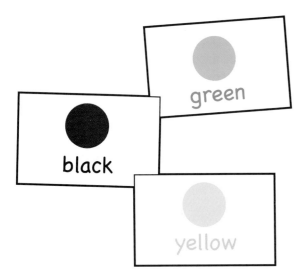

Black bear, black bear, where is your cub?

Where's the Cub?

Where is the little black bear cub? Your students will find out during this small-group activity! With students seated in a circle, place an inverted disposable bowl (cave) in front of each child. Invite a child to be the adult black bear. Direct that child to cover his eyes as you place a black pom-pom (black bear cub) under one cave and brown pom-poms (other bear cubs) under the other caves. Lead the group in chanting, "Black bear, black bear, where is your cub?" Then have the black bear choose a cave and reveal the cub. If the cub is black, the group says, "There's your black bear cub!" If it's a different color, youngsters say, "That's not a black bear cub!" and the adult black bear continues searching until the black cub is found.

Black

Flip the Feathers

For this small-group game, mix a supply of black and colorful craft feathers in a bag. Explain to youngsters that a little black hen has lost her feathers and needs their help finding them. Then hold the bag high in the air and say, "Feathers, feathers in the air, feathers flying everywhere!" and turn the bag upside down to release the feathers. After all the feathers have floated to the floor, instruct students to collect all the black feathers. When all the black feathers have been found, collect them in a pile and tell youngsters that the hen is very thankful for their help!

A Black Cat

In advance, make a simple black cat headband like the one shown. Invite a volunteer to put on the headband to play the role of the black cat. Have a small group of students stand in a circle with the black cat in the center. Tell students that this black cat only likes things that are black. Have each child, in turn, name an object. If the object is black, the black cat says, "Meow!" If the object is not black, the black cat says, "Hiss!" After each child has shared an object, invite a different student to be the black cat and continue the activity.

All Things Black

Invite little ones to put on their thinking caps for this brainstorming activity! Lead youngsters in singing and performing the song shown. At the end of the song, ask students to name other things that are black as you list their responses on chart paper.

(sung to the tune of "Skip to My Lou")

A furry black cat	*Pretend to pet a cat.*
And the black of my eye,	*Point to your eye.*
A hungry black crow	*Move fingers to resemble a beak.*
And the black night sky,	*Point at the sky.*
A black-winged bat,	*Flap your arms.*
Black ants crawling by.	*Crawl your fingers on the floor.*
What other things are black?	

Green, Green Frogs

Little ones will jump at the chance to partici-pate in this frog-themed song and activity! Place an oversize brown paper strip (log) on the floor. Invite several children to crouch on the log while holding green frog cutouts (pattern on page 59). Lead the group in singing the song shown, prompting the "frogs" to jump off the log and hop back to their seats at the appropriate time. Repeat the song several times, giving each child in the group a chance to be a frog.

(sung to the tune of the chorus of
"Jingle Bells")

Green, green frogs; green, green frogs,
Sitting on the log,
Do you see the green, green frogs
All sitting on the log?

Green, green frogs; green, green frogs,
Quick as they can be,
All jumped high up toward the sky
And got away from me!

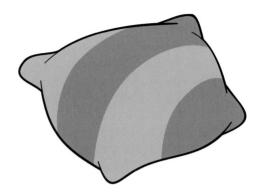

Tell Us, Please!

For this whole-group game, seat students in a circle and hand a child a small green object, such as a beanbag or a bouncy ball. To play, have youngsters pass the object around the circle as you lead them in saying the chant shown. At the end of the chant, ask the child holding the object to name something green. If desired, write the name of each item mentioned on chart paper. Then, at a later time, draw a picture or attach a magazine clipping to the chart paper to represent each word.

Tell us, please, what you have seen?
What have you seen that's the color green?

Colorful Characters

After a read-aloud of *Little Blue and Little Yellow* by Leo Lionni, give each child in a small group a white cotton ball topped with a dollop of blue paint and another cotton ball topped with a larger dollop of yellow paint. Instruct her to make her own Little Blue and Little Yellow characters hug each other until they both turn green. Then have her use the cotton balls to make prints on a sheet of paper until a desired effect is achieved.

Green

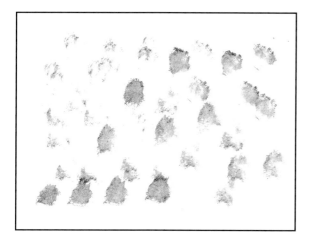

Lovely Leaves

This process art helps little ones learn about color hues! Invite a child to dab green paint in two or three different shades onto a yellow leaf cutout (patterns on page 58). Point out that although the paint colors are different shades, they are all green. Next, help him lay a sheet of waxed paper atop the leaf; then encourage him to press his hand on the paper to spread the paint. When he's finished, remove the waxed paper to reveal the leafy design. If desired, display the leaves on a paper tree and add the title "Lovely Leaves in Shades of Green!"

Step on the Goo!

Green goo? Gross! But your youngsters will purposely step on it during this large-group activity! Scatter large splotch cutouts (goo) on the floor, making most of the goo green. Play some music and have students walk around the goo. After a few moments, stop the music and prompt the group to stand on green goo. Quickly scan the group for accuracy; then have youngsters look at their shoes and prompt them to say, "Green goo on my shoes!" Restart the music to continue the game.

Orange Oranges

Engage your little ones with this sweet song and whole-group activity. Pass an uncut orange around and have youngsters examine the color of the fruit. Then slice the orange in half and show the inside of the fruit. Lead students to realize that an orange is the color orange, inside and out. Further explain that oranges are healthy snacks with many vitamins and minerals. Then lead students in singing the song shown. For added fun, after singing the song, slice a few oranges for youngsters to snack on.

(sung to the tune of "Are You Sleeping?")

Orange oranges, orange oranges,
They are sweet, good to eat,
Full of vitamin C,
And so good for me.
Orange oranges, orange oranges!

Do You Like It?

During this whole-group activity, little ones express their thoughts about orange things! Place several orange items (or pictures of orange items) in a bag. Display the bag and say the chant shown. Then take an item from the bag and display it for students. Have each child, in turn, voice his opinion about the item by saying either "I like orange [socks]; yes, I do!" or "I don't like orange [socks]; no, I do not!" Continue with the remaining items; then ask little ones to name other orange items they do or do not like.

I like the color orange; yes, I do!
I like orange things, how about you?

Colorful Produce

To prepare for this center, help youngsters brainstorm a variety of fruits and vegetables that are orange. Then place orange-tinted play dough at a center along with a small basket. A child visits the center and uses the play dough to create assorted orange produce items to fill the basket. If desired, provide the produce section of a grocery circular for students to use as a reference.

Fruity Fun

What better way to reinforce the color orange than by making an orange! For each child in a small group, cut a circle from clear, self-adhesive covering; then remove the backing and tape the circle to a tabletop sticky-side up. Instruct each child to tear orange paper scraps into small pieces and press them onto the circle, covering its surface. When each youngster is finished, help her trim any excess paper from the edge. For added fun, spray each project with citrus-scented air freshener or body spray. Then display these aromatic crafts on a tree cutout with the title "These Oranges Are the Pick of the Crop!"

Blending Buddies

To begin, brush red paint onto white paper and then tell youngsters you're going to turn the red paint orange! Have students observe as you blend yellow paint with the red paint. Ask students to describe what happens. After children respond that the paint turned orange, pair students and give each twosome a red crayon, a yellow crayon, and a sheet of white paper. Encourage each student to draw or scribble on the paper, overlapping the colors and observing what happens. Finally, have each child share his observations about color mixing with the group.

In the Bag

Little ones need their thinking caps for this whole-group game! Place unrelated brown items—such as a Lincoln Logs piece, a potato, a crayon, a teddy bear, and sandpaper—in a paper grocery bag. To begin, remove an item from the bag and have youngsters identify it. Invite students to tell something about the item; then place it on the floor in plain view. Repeat the process with each remaining item. After all the items have been revealed, ask, "What one thing is the same about all the items?" leading youngsters to discover that the items are all the color brown.

Chocolate Cone

Little ones are sure to agree—a chocolate ice cream cone is a tasty example of the color brown! To make this delicious-looking craft, thicken white paint with flour and then tint the mixture with chocolate syrup. Set out the mixture, a paint brush, chocolate candy sprinkles, glue, and a class supply of tagboard cones and ice cream scoops. Invite each child to glue an ice cream scoop to a cone. Then have her paint the scoop with the mixture, encouraging her to smell the chocolaty scent as she works. Before the mixture dries, have her top the ice cream scoop with chocolate sprinkles!

Find Them All

Color recognition is the key to this fast-paced game. Gather pairs of similar items, with one item in each pair being brown and the other item a different color. (See the list for suggested items.) Then place the items on a tray. Explain that to play the game, children may only remove the brown items from the tray. Then set a timer and say to a child, "Find the brown [item name]!" After the child removes the correct item from the tray, announce another brown item. Continue until all the brown items are removed or time runs out. Give the player a high five for a job well done and then ready the tray for another round.

Suggested pairs of items: feathers, pom-poms, crayons, markers, paper strips, yarn

Brown Is All Around!

Secretly stage your group area with brown objects that can be viewed easily. Lead youngsters in singing the song shown. At the end of the song, help students notice classmates or adults who have brown hair and eyes. Then encourage little ones to scan the area to find other items that are the color brown.

(sung to the tune of "The Wheels on the Bus")

Brown is all around; look up and down,
Brown hair and eyes,
Brown trees and ground.
Brown is all around; look left and right.
Brown is within your sight!

Splash!

With this small-group color-recognition game, youngsters jump in the mud without getting messy! Gather color cards, ensuring that a few cards are brown. Place an oversize brown paper mud puddle on the floor and have youngsters stand around the edge. Display a card. If the color shown is brown, little ones jump in the mud and stomp their feet. If it's a different color, students stand still. Repeat for several rounds, picking a new card each time.

See pages 61–63 for a reproducible booklet that targets color skills!

My Circle!

Youngsters learn some basic characteristics of circles as they sing this toe-tapping tune. To begin, give each child a colorful sheet of paper and have her draw a point in the center of it. Then demonstrate how to draw a curved line around the center point, emphasizing how the two ends of the curved line meet up. Guide each youngster to draw a circle around the center point on her paper in the same manner. Then have students cut out their circles. Lead students in singing the song shown, encouraging them to use their circle cutouts to point out the characteristics of circles mentioned in the song.

(sung to the tune of "Clementine")

Oh, my circle!
Oh, my circle!
Oh, my circle, round and neat!
You keep curving round the middle,
And your two ends always meet!

Pretty Prints

Students make circle prints of all different sizes at this art center! In advance, gather a variety of items that make a circle print, such as cardboard tubes; paper cups; jar lids; or clean, empty shampoo bottles. Place the items at a center along with paper and shallow containers of paint. A child chooses an item and dips the rim in a container of paint. Then he gently presses the rim of the item on the paper. He continues in this manner using different items and different colors of paint until a desired effect is achieved. When each child is done with his project, challenge him to count the number of circle prints he made on his paper.

Point It Out

Students learn to recognize circles when they participate in this small-group activity! Display several large shape cutouts, making sure that a few of the shapes are circles. Review the shape names with a small group of students. Then lead the group in the chant shown. At the end of the chant, invite a volunteer to point to a circle. If she is correct, remove the circle she pointed to. Continue in this manner with different volunteers until all of the circles have been located. For an added challenge, display circles of various sizes and colors. Include a descriptor in the chant, such as "Point to a small circle" or "Point to a red circle." Then have students find the circle that matches the description.

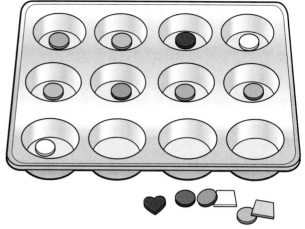

Where is a circle?
Where can one be?
Point to a circle
So we can all see!

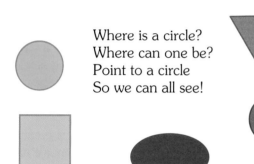

Sweet Circles

Yum! Sorting shapes has never been more delicious! At a center, place a muffin tin and a supply of craft foam shapes. Ensure that there is exactly one circle for each section of the muffin tin. A child visits the center and looks through the shapes. When he finds a circle, he puts it in a section of the muffin tin. He continues until he has placed one circle in each section of the muffin tin. For added fun, have the child pretend to bake the treats and then "serve" them to his classmates.

Hop, Jump, or Crawl!

Encourage students to get moving with this gross-motor activity! Gather students in an open area, making sure there is plenty of space between each child. Then announce an action (see the suggested movements) and encourage each student to move his body in a small circle using the action given. Continue in this manner, announcing several different actions for students to perform. To conclude the activity, direct youngsters to join hands to form a large circle.

Suggested movements: spinning, hopping, walking forward, walking backward, jumping, crawling, skipping, stomping

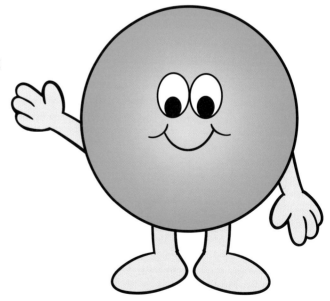

Equal Sides

Showcase the fact that a square has four sides of the same length with this lively song. Display an oversize square cutout; then lead students in singing the song shown. After singing the song, display the square again and use a ruler or a yardstick to demonstrate that all four sides are the same length. Next, show students a variety of four-sided shape cutouts, some of which are squares. Invite student volunteers, in turn, to point out each square.

(sung to the tune of
"This Old Man")

Look right there
And compare;
Equal sides make up a square.
All four sides are the same.
That seems very fair!
Equal sides make up a square.

Square Dance!

In advance, use masking tape to make a large square on the floor in an open area. Also stack several copies of the shape cards from page 64 facedown nearby. Have students stand around the large square and invite a child to choose a shape card. If she picks a square card, she calls out, "Square dance!" Play some lively music and have students dance around the square until the music stops. If the child chooses a card that is not a square, she returns the card facedown to the bottom of the stack. Invite different students to choose cards and continue in this manner as time permits.

Side by Side

Youngsters build squares, one side at a time! Cut same-color pipe cleaners to make four equal-size pieces. Make several similar sets in different lengths and colors. Gather a small group of students and randomly arrange the pipe cleaners in front of the group. Challenge the group to work together to use the pipe cleaner pieces to build as many squares as they can, reminding students that a square has four corners and four equal sides. When the group has finished, count the sides on each square, in turn, verifying that the sides are equal in length.

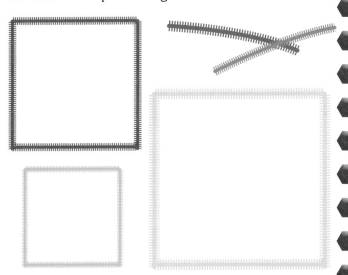

Square

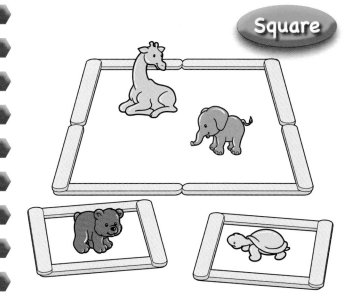

Animal Pens

At a center, place a supply of craft sticks and several plastic animal toys. Tell youngsters to pretend that the animals at this center live at a special zoo. Further explain that each animal at this zoo must live in a square-shaped pen. A child visits the center and uses the craft sticks to build a separate square pen for each animal. Then challenge students to use the craft sticks to make different-size square pens for the animals, putting more than one animal in some of the larger pens.

Big and Small

Squares can be many different sizes, as your students will discover when they go on this square hunt! Show students a medium-size tagboard square and have them name the shape. Then encourage youngsters to look around the classroom and find other squares. When a student finds a square, hold the tagboard square next to the object to confirm that it is a square. Then lead students in the chant shown. For an added challenge, have students decide whether the featured object is smaller, larger, or the same size as the tagboard square.

A [name of item] is a square,
Yes, indeed!
How many more squares do we see?

Is It a Triangle?

For this whole-group activity, cut out several copies of the shape cards from page 64, making sure that many of the shapes are triangles. Put the cards in a bag. Also program a two-column chart as shown. Review the number of sides that different shapes have. Then have youngsters pass the bag around the circle as you lead them in saying the chant. At the end of the chant, prompt the child holding the bag to take a card. Help him count the sides of the shape to confirm whether or not it is a triangle; then have him attach the card to the appropriate column on the chart. Continue until the bag is empty.

We'll pull a shape and count to see
If its sides will number three!

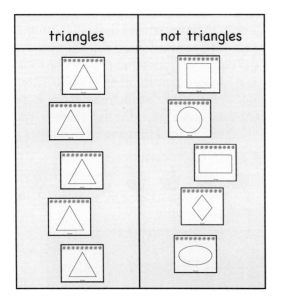

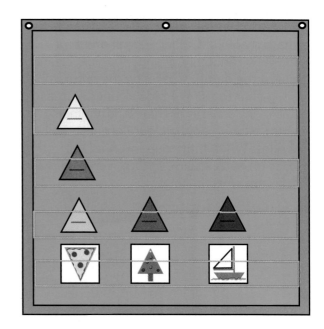

Simply the Best

To prepare for this pocket chart activity, place pictures or simple drawings of three triangular objects—such as a pizza slice, Christmas tree, and sailboat—in the bottom row. Give each child a personalized triangle cutout (or triangle card from page 64) and point out how each pictured item on the chart is triangular. Then ask each student, in turn, to place her triangle in the pocket chart above the triangular item she likes the best. After all the triangles are in place, discuss the results with students.

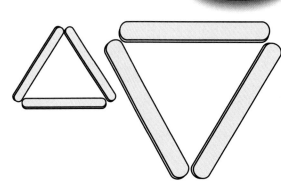

Where's a Triangle?

With this simple song and activity little ones demonstrate that a triangle has three sides! Give each child a triangle cutout and help her identify the shape. Then have her place the triangle on the floor and trace each side with her finger. Ask, "How many sides does a triangle have?" After confirming that a triangle has three sides, instruct youngsters to hold the shapes behind their backs. Lead the group in singing the song, prompting students to show the triangles at the appropriate time.

(sung to the tune of "Where Is Thumbkin?")

Where's a triangle, where's a triangle?
There are three sides you'll see.
Here is a triangle, here is a triangle.
There are three sides I see!

Big and Small

Invite a small group of children to join you at your math center. Give each child three small craft sticks and three jumbo craft sticks. Also keep three of each size for yourself. Demonstrate how to make a triangle using the small craft sticks; then encourage youngsters to do the same. When everyone is finished, have students count the sides and then the corners to see that there are three of each. Next, use the jumbo craft sticks to make a triangle in a different orientation than the first one. Have youngsters follow suit; then point out that although the sizes and orientations of the triangles are different, the shape remains the same.

Three Sides and Three Corners

For this small-group activity, cut a length of yarn several feet long and tie the loose ends together. Then invite three children to turn the yarn into a triangle. To do so, have the children stand and face each other. Help each child hook an index finger around the yarn; then direct the children to slowly back away from one another to create a triangle. After a triangle is formed, lead students in walking around the shape and counting the three sides. Then point out that the three corners of the triangle are formed where the youngsters are holding the yarn.

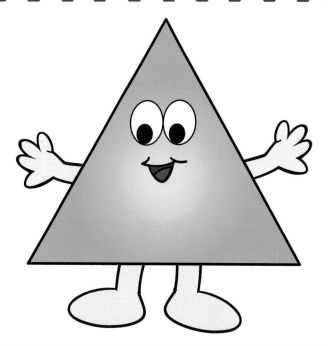

Rectangles, Rectangles

To introduce this song and activity, display a copy of the rectangle card on page 64, pointing out the two long sides and two short sides of the shape. Then focus youngsters' attention on a classroom door. Ask, "Is the shape of the door similar to the shape of a rectangle?" After youngsters respond, pose a similar question about the shape of a bed. Then lead little ones in singing the song shown. At the end of the song, help students brainstorm other rectangle-shaped objects.

(sung to the tune of "Skip to My Lou")

Rectangles, rectangles, I see you.
A door is a rectangle; this is true.
My cozy bed and my pillow too—
Rectangles, I see you!

Window Watching

To prepare for this art center activity, cut strips of colorful paper in two different lengths. Also provide light-color construction paper, markers, and glue. Instruct a child to take two strips of each size and arrange them on a sheet of paper to form a rectangular window. After arranging the strips, have her glue them in place. Then encourage her to imagine she is looking out a window at home. Encourage her to draw a picture of what she might see when she looks out that window. If desired, attach youngsters' completed projects to a display titled "Look Out the Window. What Do We See?"

Rectangle

What a Robot!

Inspire your little ones to create a robot using only rectangles! Set out a variety of colorful paper rectangles, craft foam rectangles, and tagboard rectangles. Invite a youngster to visit the area and use the items to create a robot on a sheet of paper. When she is satisfied with her work, have her glue the pieces in place. If desired, help each child determine how many rectangles she used to make her robot and label her project with a sentence like the one shown.

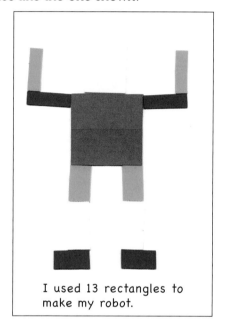

I used 13 rectangles to make my robot.

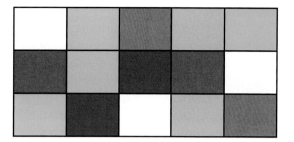

Handmade Quilt

For this whole-group activity, cut out an oversize paper rectangle (quilt base) and gather enough colorful construction paper rectangles (quilt pieces) to cover the base. Place the base on the floor and have youngsters identify the shape. Then give each child a quilt piece, leading him to notice that it is also rectangular, just a different size. To assemble the quilt, lead youngsters in the chant shown. Then invite a child to place his quilt piece on the base, helping him position it. Continue in the same way until each child has added a piece to the quilt.

Colorful pieces for a quilt,
Let's work together and get it built!

Sit and Switch

Instead of a circle-time game, invite little ones to play a rectangle-time game! Attach an oversize masking tape rectangle on the floor. Before seating students, walk along the rectangle and point out its two long and two short sides. Then instruct youngsters to sit on the rectangle, facing out. To play the game, hand one child a construction paper rectangle. Have her walk around the group saying, "Rectangle, rectangle, rectangle, shape!" Then have her drop the rectangle in the closest classmate's lap. Direct both children to walk around the rectangle, switching seats before they sit down. Then hand the rectangle to a different child and continue play until everyone has switched seats.

A Special Tree

Help children differentiate shapes with this easy-to-prepare activity. Cut out green construction paper shapes, making most of the shapes ovals. Mount a paper tree without foliage to a wall and place the shapes nearby. Lead youngsters in reciting the chant shown. At the end of the chant, ask a child to take a shape. If the shape is an oval, have her attach it to the tree. If it's a different shape, have her set it aside. Continue until all ovals are hanging on the tree.

This is a special tree, you see.
It only has oval-shaped leaves!

Squeeze and Stamp

Help students see the difference between ovals and circles using a cardboard tube! To prepare for this center, cut a cardboard tube into several shorter lengths. Set out the tubes along with shallow containers of paint and a supply of paper. Display a tube, drawing youngsters' attention to the circle-shaped opening. Then gently squeeze the sides of the tube so that the opening is an oval shape. Give each child a tube and encourage her to squeeze the sides to make the circular opening into an oval. While she squeezes the sides of the tube, direct the child to lightly dip it in a container of paint and then make oval prints on a sheet of paper.

Impressive Ovals

Fill your sensory table or a large plastic tub with very moist sand. Provide laminated tagboard oval cutouts in assorted sizes. Invite a child to lay an oval on the sand and then use his finger to trace around the outline. Encourage him to repeat the process with other ovals to make tracings in various sizes. When he's finished, have him smooth out the sand with his hand.

What's an Oval Shaped Like?

To prepare for this song, show students an oval cutout or draw a large oval on the board. Have youngsters identify the shape. Then lead students in singing the song shown.

(sung to the tune of "Did You Ever See a Lassie?")

Did you ever see an oval,
An oval, an oval?
Did you ever see an oval?
I'll show one to you!

You'll notice it's shaped like
An egg or a green grape.
Did you ever see an oval?
I'll show one to you!

Just Awesome!

Little ones identify ovals as they burn off extra energy with this activity! Make a class supply of large oval cutouts plus a few cutouts that are other shapes. Arrange the cutouts on the floor in an oval shape. Have each child stand beside a shape. Then play some music and have students march along the shapes. Stop the music and have youngsters stop near the closest shape. Prompt each child who is standing closest to an oval to say, "Ovals are awesome!" Have each child who is standing on a different shape hand it to you and then move to an unoccupied oval. Restart the music and repeat the activity until only ovals are left. Then conclude the activity by having everyone say, "Ovals are awesome!"

Jazzy Jewelers

For this whole-group activity, transform several pipe cleaners into individual rings. For each ring, cut out a white tagboard diamond; then place the diamonds in a bag with several different tagboard shapes. Seat students in a circle and place the rings on the floor. Pretend to be a jeweler and tell little ones you need help fitting each ring with the perfect diamond. Then lead youngsters in saying the chant shown as they pass the bag around the circle. At the end of the chant, have the child with the bag remove a shape and tell if it's a diamond. If the shape is a diamond, have her place it above a ring. If it's not a diamond, have her set it aside. Continue until each ring has a diamond.

We can't fit these rings with just anything.
They are special-order diamond rings!

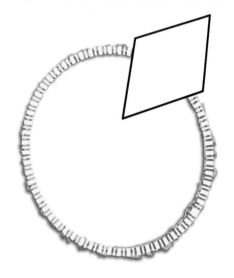

Dazzling Design

For this small-group activity, provide a supply of same-size colorful diamond cutouts and a jumbo die. Have a child roll the die, count the dots, and take that many diamonds from the supply. Encourage him to begin a design by joining the diamonds together along the sides. Then invite a different child in the group to repeat the process, adding to the design. Continue in the same way until all the diamonds are used.

Diamond

Digging for Diamonds

Bury a supply of craft foam shapes in your sand table, making sure most of the shapes are diamonds. Provide a small plastic shovel and a treasure chest. Invite youngsters to visit the area and pretend they are diamond mining. Each time a child discovers a diamond, have him put it in the treasure chest. When he digs up a different shape, have him set it aside.

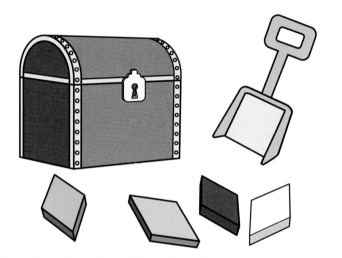

Around the Bases

While playing this small-group game, little ones get plenty of practice with shape recognition and formation. To prepare, make an oversize masking tape diamond (baseball diamond) on the floor. Gather assorted shape cards (page 64), including several diamonds. Invite four students to stand on different points (bases) on the baseball diamond. Explain that, in this game, players move to the next base each time you hold up a card that shows a diamond. Then display a card. If the card shows a diamond, players move to the next base. If it shows a different shape, players stay on their current base. Play continues until each child returns to his original base.

Diamond in the Sky

To prepare for this song and activity, invite each child to decorate a construction paper diamond (kite) with markers and a crepe paper streamer. Lead youngsters in singing the song, encouraging each child to use her kite to perform the actions. At the end of the song, invite each youngster to tell what might happen if her kite gets blown away by a mighty wind. If desired, write each child's response on separate paper and have her illustrate the page. Then bind the pages together to make a class book titled "Blown Away!"

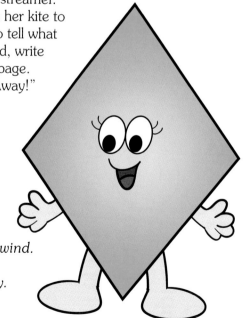

(sung to the tune of "The Farmer in the Dell")

A diamond in the sky,
A diamond in the sky,
My kite is way up high,
A diamond in the sky.

Pretend to fly your kite.

Continue flying your kite.

A mighty wind blows by.
A mighty wind blows by.
My diamond's sailing off
Into the clear blue sky!

Pretend the kite gets blown by the wind.

Lower your kite and look at the sky.

Direction Cards

Use with "Candy Kiss Cookie" on page 6.

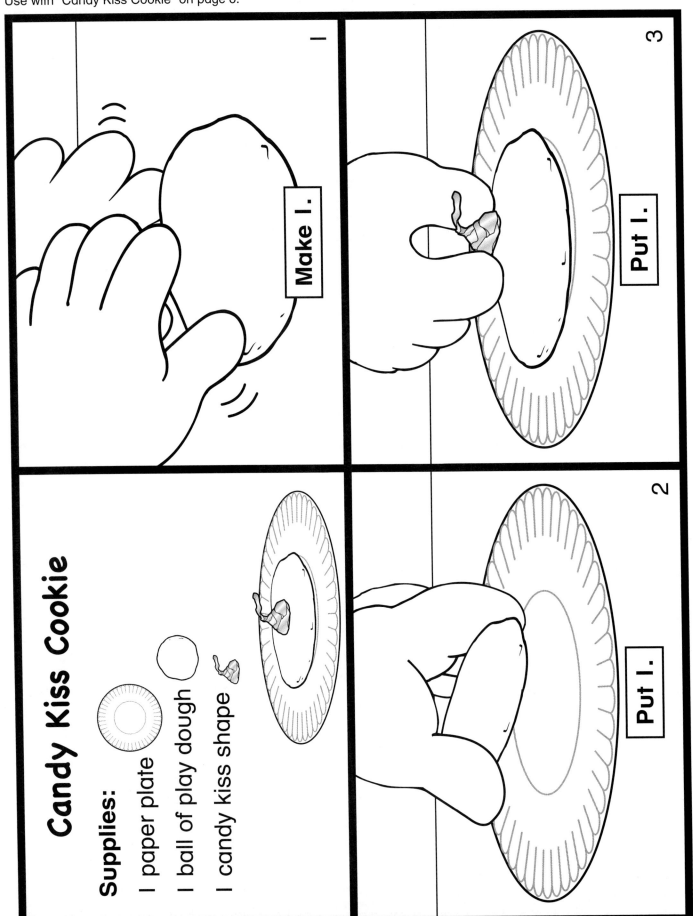

Candy Kiss Cookie

Supplies:

1 paper plate

1 ball of play dough

1 candy kiss shape

1   Make 1.

2   Put 1.

3   Put 1.

TEC61428

TEC61428

TEC61428

TEC61428

TEC61428

TEC61428

TEC61428

TEC61428

TEC61428

TEC61428

TEC61428

TEC61428

Traffic Light Pattern
Use with "A Traffic Light Has Three" on page 10.

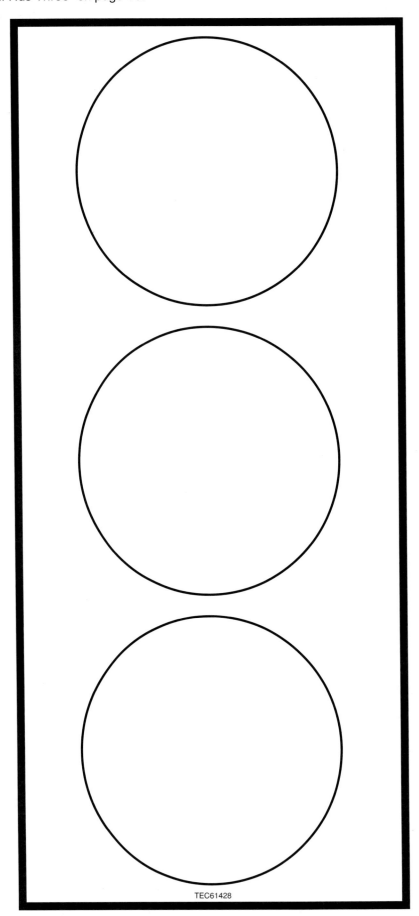

TEC61428

We ♥ Numbers, Colors, & Shapes • ©The Mailbox® Books • TEC61428

Where's the Cheese?

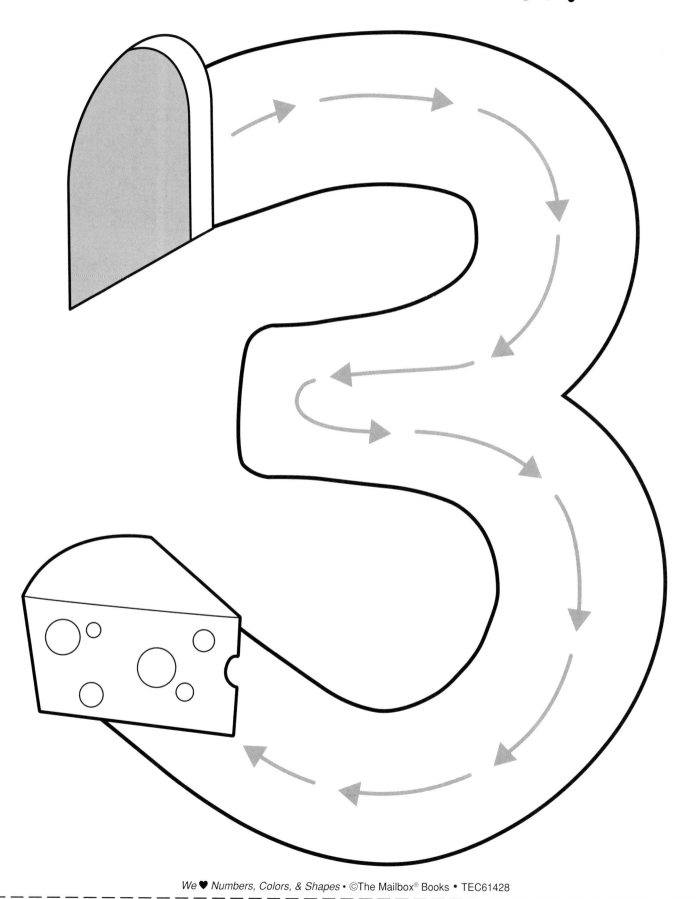

Note to the teacher: Use with "Three Blind Mice" on page 11.

Leaf Patterns
Use with "Leaf Expedition" on page 11 and "Lovely Leaves" on page 37.

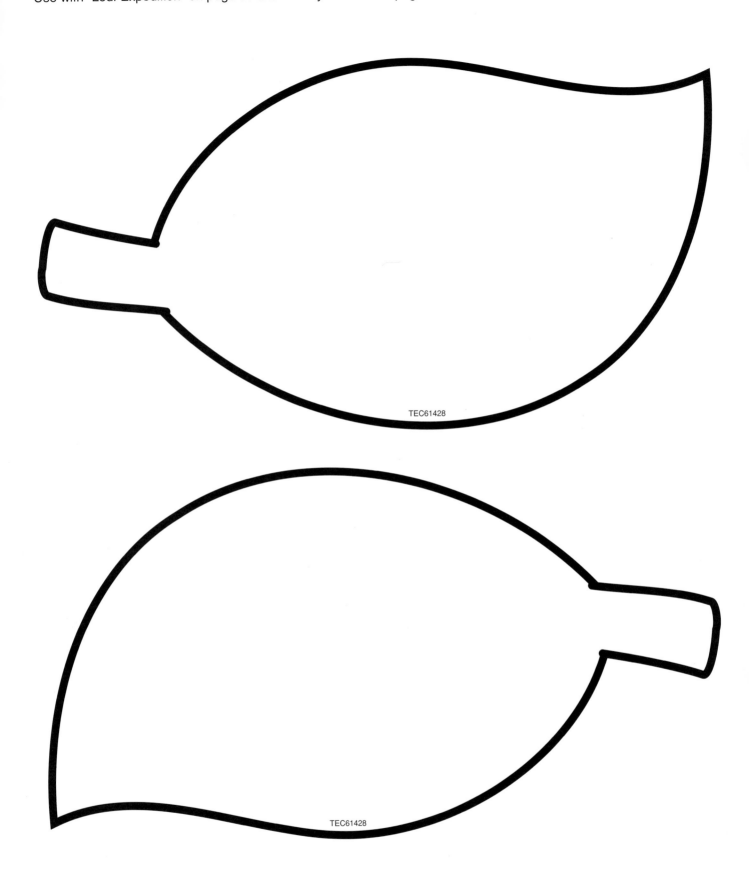

TEC61428

TEC61428

We ♥ Numbers, Colors, & Shapes • ©The Mailbox® Books • TEC61428

TEC61428

60

Note to the teacher: Use with "How Many Cherries?" on page 14.

Directions: Use this page with pages 62 and 63. Help each child cut out the picture cards and the booklet cover and pages. Next, help her glue each card to the appropriate page; then read the color word on each page and encourage her to color the splotch with a matching color crayon. Stack the booklet cover and pages in order and staple them along the left side.

Cat's Colors

Name _____

We ♥ Numbers, Colors, & Shapes • ©The Mailbox® Books • TEC61428

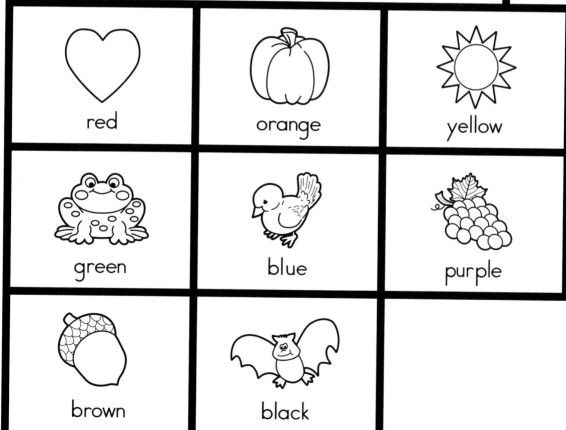

red

orange

yellow

green

blue

purple

brown

black

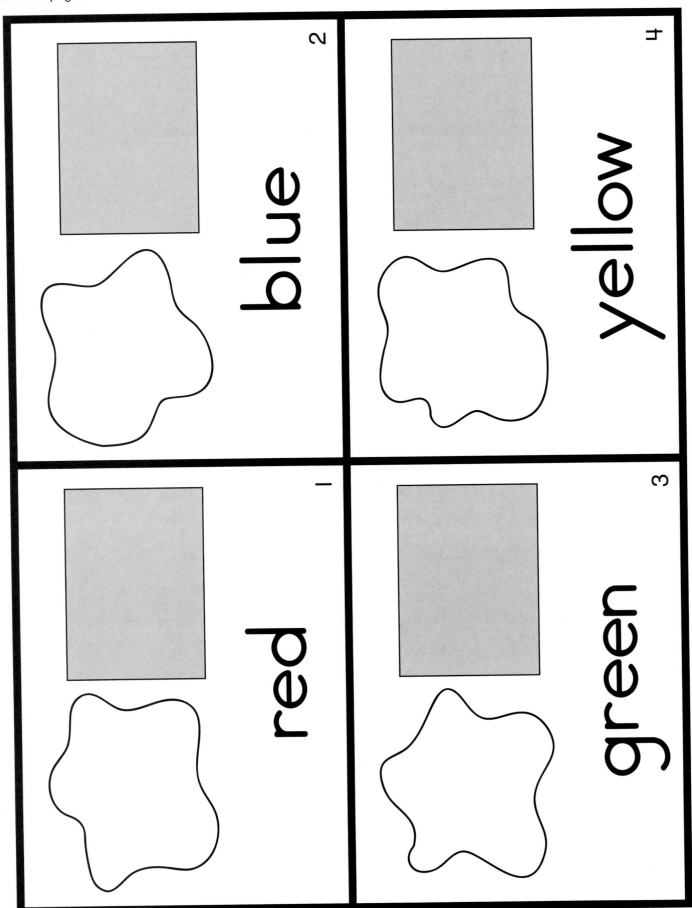

blue

2

yellow

4

red

1

green

3

We ♥ Numbers, Colors, & Shapes • ©The Mailbox® Books • TEC61428

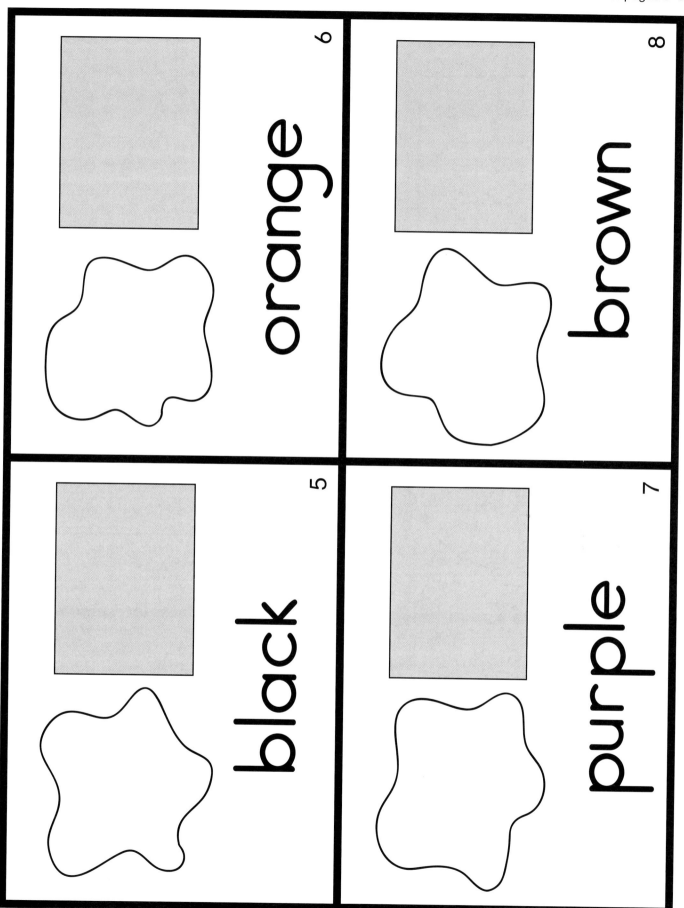

6

orange

8

brown

5

black

7

purple

Shape Cards

Use with "Square Dance!" on page 44, "Is It a Triangle?" on page 46, "Rectangles, Rectangles" on page 48, and "Around the Bases" on page 53.

TEC61428

TEC61428

TEC61428

TEC61428

TEC61428

TEC61428

We ♥ Numbers, Colors, & Shapes • ©The Mailbox® Books • TEC61428

It starts with
ONE.

We know the difference one can make.

One happy getting-to-know you song that makes everyone feel included.

One circle time activity that turns off their shyness and turns on their curiosity.

One handmade craft that stays in a family for years (because macaroni has serious longevity).

These experiences define childhood, and shaping young lives is why we love to teach.

We're in the business of giving teachers what they need. Together, we can be the difference.

Visit **TheMailbox.com** to find out how.

The **MAILBOX**®
Be the Difference®

Preschool

We ♥ Numbers, Colors, & Shapes

The MAILBOX

TEC61428

Preschoolers love to learn! *We ♥ Numbers, Colors, & Shapes* features fun, practical, and developmentally appropriate activities to help your little ones learn early math skills. What's not to love about that?

Group-time ideas

Circle

Songs

Center ideas

Art activities

Helpful reproducibl[e]

Other Books in the We ♥ Series:

TEC61425. We ♥ Alphabet • Preschool

TEC61426. We ♥ Themes • Preschool

TEC61427. We ♥ Science • Preschool

TEC61429. We ♥ Seasons & Holidays • Preschool

TheMailbox.com

ISBN 978-161276482

9 781612 764825

About This Book

Don't let another month catch you by surprise! The Ready for... monthly books are packed with just-for-preschool ideas on the monthly themes your students love most. As an extra bonus, they also include colorful teaching tools to tear out and use. Ready for a new month? You bet!

Themes included in this book:
- Snow and Mittens
- Penguins
- Dental Health
- Valentine's Day
...and more!

Other Books in the Ready For... monthly books series:

TEC61417. Ready for September & October • Preschool
TEC61418. Ready for November & December • Preschool
TEC61420. Ready for March, April, & May • Preschool

If you have a book idea, we'd like to hear from you. See www.themailbox.com for submission guidelines.

THE MAILBOX Book Company®

We Started With Teachers and Their Students
- Teachers Jake and Marge Michel started The Education Center, Inc., publishing company in the basement of their North Carolina home. Their first product was a set of teacher idea cards stored in a cute canvas bag.
- In 1979, Jake and Marge started a new magazine comprised of ideas sent in by kindergarten–grade 6 teachers. It was called *The Mailbox*. Teachers loved it. Before long, *The Mailbox* was being used in classrooms by hundreds of thousands of teachers.
- Today *The Mailbox* is published in five editions, along with *Teacher's Helper*® magazine (two editions).

We're Still All About Teachers and Their Students
- At The Mailbox Books, we understand that every minute counts in today's classroom. We've studied the state and national standards you are being held accountable for. From this research, we've identified the key skills students at your grade level are being required to learn. We build our books around these skills so that you can use them with the confidence that they'll help you reach your teaching goals.
- The Mailbox Books now offers over 450 titles for preschool–grade 6 teachers. These books can be found in over 1,000 teacher stores around the world.

The
MAILBOX.